What Do We Know About Matter?

 HOUGHTON MIFFLIN HARCOURT

PHOTOGRAPHY CREDITS: (c) ©Digital Vision/Getty Images; 3 (c) ©Alamy Images Royalty Free; 5 (t) ©Yagi Studio/Photodisc/Getty Images; 7 (tr) ©Lawren Lu/Cutcaster; 7 (tl) ©Comstock Images/Getty Images; 7 (bl) ©Fuse/Getty Images; 7 (br) ©Ilene MacDonald/Alamy Images; 8 (b) ©Foodcollection.com/Alamy; 9 (b) ©Zoom Team/Shutterstock; 10 (b) ©Joel Sartore/National Geographic/Getty Images; 11 ©Serge Krouglikoff/Digital Vision/Getty Images

Printed in Mexico

ISBN: 978-0-5440-7210-7

2 3 4 5 6 7 8 9 10 0908 21 20 19 18 17 16 15 14 13

4500456309   A B C D E F G

Look for each word in yellow along with its meaning.

matter	texture	melt
property	temperature	evaporate
weight	freeze	condense

Underlined sentences answer these questions.

What is matter?

What makes matter different?

How can we measure and classify matter?

What happens when you cool or heat matter?

What happens when water evaporates or vapor condenses?

What is matter?

Matter is anything that takes up space. Your milk and plate are matter. Your lunch is matter. You are matter!

The table is matter. The chair is, too.

sandwich

glass

plate

milk

3

What makes matter different?

Matter has different properties. A property is one part of what something is like.

Weight is the measure of how heavy matter feels. Texture is how matter feels. Weight and texture are properties.

Size, color, and shape are properties, too.

The new glue changed the texture of the paper.

Sometimes scientists work with matter to make new things. A scientist made a new type of glue. He put it on some small pieces of paper. He made sticky notes. Now the paper can stick to things.

How can we measure and classify matter?

We can use tools to measure matter. We can measure a desk. We use a ruler to measure a desk. We can measure you with a ruler, too! A thermometer measures how hot and cold things are.

A scale is a tool. It tells how much you weigh.

scale

We can make groups of matter with similar properties.

Which animal is heavy?

bear

butterfly

Which building is tall?

dog house

skyscr

What happens when you cool or heat matter?

You can cool water. Its temperature will change. Temperature is a measure of how hot or cold something is. The water can freeze into ice. Some other types of matter freeze, too.

Water freezes into ice when it is cooled.

Ice is matter. Put some ice in the hot sun. The ice will melt into liquid water. Some matter changes when you heat it.

The ice will turn back into liquid water.

What happens when water evaporates or vapor condenses?

Water will evaporate when heat is added. To evaporate means to change from a liquid to a gas. The stove changes the water as it heats it. The water turns into a gas in the air. This gas is called water vapor.

Water evaporates into the air.

Water vapor condenses when it is cooled. To condense means to change from a gas to a liquid. The cold glass cools water vapor in the air. The water vapor condenses as drops of water on the glass.

Change Matter

Have an adult help you warm some butter. You can use a microwave or the warm sun. Then put the butter in the freezer. Look at it the next day. Talk about what happened.

 ## Name the Properties

Look at something in your classroom. Tell a partner about the object's properties. What color is the object? How does it feel? What shape is it? Is it heavy? Can your partner guess what it is? Draw a picture of it.